A Basic Guide to Lesson Planning for Teacher Candidates and Beginning Teachers

By Felicia Moss Mayfield EdD

ISBN 978-1-7345482-0-4 (Paperback)

ISBN 978-1-1-7345482-1 (Digital)

This workbook belongs to:

_____

Date_____

Introduction

Similar to many college instructors who look for a product to facilitate learning in their classroom, I simply did not find one that matches the learning needs of my students. Furthermore, I wanted to build on the expectations of the INTASC standards (2019) particularly Standards 6, 7 and 8. An instructive product which would focus on writing practice lesson plans was not at my search engine fingertips. Something was needed. So, I asked, "If I were an undergraduate student learning how to write lesson plans, what would help me?" When new teacher candidates enter the field, a simple old school consumable workbook was needed to be both instructive, while providing opportunities for practice. Since paper is losing widespread respect for delivery of instructional material, this will be an online workbook as well.

This book is written for the thousands of hope-filled prospective teachers who believe they can make a difference. After 45 school years, I believe I can *still* make a difference. That is why I am composing this workbook in beta form for teacher candidates who will be in my class this semester. I simply did not find the product which I was looking for. So, I started to design what I needed to teach how to develop a lesson plan. You could say that this is a unit or module within my course. True to my craft there are six easy lessons about lesson plans within this module. Modeling and demonstrating...my craft!

Felicia, teacher

TABLE OF CONTENTS

Lesson 1

What is a Lesson Plan?

Instructional Content

A **lesson plan** is a **design which provides** a meaningful plan of action to produce learning using information and experiences provided by the teacher for the learner(s) during a typical class period.

A lesson plan design is analogous to the following:

teacher: lesson plan~ architect: blueprint

teacher: lesson plan~ coach: game plan

teacher: lesson plan~ project manager: PMP

· ·
Your turn

Select the correct choice

Teacher: lesson plan~ doctor: a. chart b. nurse c. medicine d. Epi-pen

Correct. A. The chart, which is now electronic in most cases, is the plan for healing or maintenance of wellness.
· ·

Practitioner's testimonial

"As a 45-year educator, I have seen a shift from a lesson plan with steps to teaching, to more recently a design to promote learning. The former lesson plan was teacher focused. The intent was to be thorough. There was a benign list of materials, steps, under the heading of a measurable objective. Now, a good lesson plan is a design. A design is an intentional plan with a focus on outcomes for the consumer (Schlechty, 2019). The teacher, therefore, is not doing a performance, but is designing and shaping cognition. This is noninvasive brain surgery." Felicia, teacher

Lesson 1 Practice

What is a lesson plan?

A lesson plan is a design for teachers to teach and students to learn.

What is a lesson plan?

Search for at least three other definitions on the web and write what you find. Include the authors' names, and/or the link:

_____

_____

_____

_____

What are some of the common elements that you found with the three or more of the definitions? What are some differences? Complete the chart below.

Compare	Contrast

Evaluation:

In your own words, give an operational definition of a lesson plan.

NOTES for Lesson 1

Using the Cornell Model*

Key Words	Key Ideas

Summary:

*A design by Walter Paulk, a professor at Cornell University *Pauk, Walter; Owens, Ross J. Q. (2010). How to Study in College (10 ed.). Boston, MA: Wadsworth. ISBN 978-1-4390-8446-5.* Chapter 10: "The Cornell System: Take Effective Notes", pp. 235-277

LESSON 2

The Parts of a Lesson Plan

Instructional Content

1. WHO? Who are the students? What grade level? Subject? Who is the teacher? What is the cultural context? Am I relevant and responsive? **See Culturally Relevant/Culturally Responsive Pedagogy CRP** (Ladson-Billing, 1995) (Gay, 2002)

2. WHAT? What you are teaching is broadly referred to as the subject or content. Specifically, it is referred to as the **Standard**, objective, content, focus, subject, etc.

3. WHEN? What period, audience or time period is this class? Is it part of a longer **unit**, **module** or **learning segment**?

4. WHERE? Is this experience totally in the classroom? Virtual?

5. HOW? What will the delivery of this lesson look like? What materials will you need to teach this lesson? A textbook? eBook? Which pages? A read aloud? Safety goggles for all students? A lab to demonstrate safe use of a Bunsen burner? Being prepared is key to the success of any activity.

6. The start is key. There are many names for what the beginning of the lesson is called: anticipatory set, creating the atmosphere, getting the attention of the learning. They all fall under the category of starting

the lesson. For this exercise we will unify the nomenclature and simply call it "The Beginning". The body of the lesson with clear steps will be called simply, "The Middle." The closing of the lesson will be called "The Ending."

Read about the importance of getting students ready to learn. https://teach.com/what/teachers-change-lives/motivating-students/

As prospective teachers or beginning teachers, you will be taught how to do lesson planning by veterans who may have been under the tutelage of Madeline Hunter (Hunter, 2004). Hunter refers to the beginning as the **anticipatory set**.

Lesson 2 The Parts of a Lesson Plan

Lesson Plan

Date _____

Teacher's Name _____ School _____ Class Time/Period _____

Subject _____ Students _____

Focus of the Lesson and GSE Standard _____

Class Announcements, Taking Roll, and Removal of all Barriers to Learning

Beginning—Introduction/Engagement/Grabbing Interest/Bridging from the last lesson and prior knowledge, What do the students already know? Have I addressed Maslow's Hierarchy of needs? Create the Experience.

_____

Academic Language needed _____

Materials needed _____

Technology needed _____

ISTE Standard Addressed

Middle—Methods, Activities, Steps

1. Communicate the focus of the day's lesson and purpose

2. Review the vocabulary, materials and resources needed to be successful

3. Present the new information—Differentiate with questioning and delivery. Ask what am I providing for those on grade level? Below grade level? Above grade level? _____

   _____

4. Model the appropriate response

5. Give opportunities for practice—Differentiate with the expected outcome

End—Closure and Summary of the Lesson

1. Are the students able to share what they learned?

2. Gather evidence of learning _____

3. Assign homework or some method of reinforcing the learning, as well as setting the stage for what is to come.

Reflection—Did the students learn the material? Why? Why not? What do I need to adjust? What ISTE Teacher Standard did you use while preparing and teaching this lesson?

Felicia Moss Mayfield Ed.D.©

Lesson 2 The Parts of a Lesson Plan

Practice

What part of the lesson plan template refers to the WHO?

_____

_____

What parts of the lesson plan template refer to the WHAT? (Hint: standard, focus of the lesson)

_____

What parts of the lesson plan template refer to the WHEN? (Hint: period, length of lesson) _____

What parts of the lesson plan template refer to the HOW? (Hint: materials technology, assessment)

_____

_____

When we talk about WHO we must ensure we are taking into account the cultural context of the students. The WHO is not just a grade level or a section of freshman algebra. The WHO is considering the universe of the **whole child** (ASCD, 2019). The students, their diversity, and planning a lesson that ensures respect of culture and heritage.

When we talk about the WHAT, It must be understood that a standard is a broad statement of content. There is much unpacking inside of any standard to address specific essential questions of inquiry. There is a world of knowledge and content inside of each standard (Harris, 2019). For this exercise, we are looking for the broad content and focus of the lesson.

NOTES for Lesson 2

Using the Cornell Model*

Key Words	Key Ideas

Summary:

*A design by Walter Paulk, a professor at Cornell University *Pauk, Walter; Owens, Ross J. Q. (2010). How to Study in College (10 ed.). Boston, MA: Wadsworth. ISBN 978-1-4390-8446-5.* Chapter 10: "The Cornell System: Take Effective Notes", pp. 235-277

Lesson 3

The Beginning

Instructional Content

Lesson Plan

Date _____

Teacher's Name _____ School _____ Class Time _____

Subject _____

Focus of the Lesson and GSE Standard _____

Class Announcements, Taking Roll, and Removal of all Barriers to Learning

Beginning—Introduction/Engagement/Grabbing Interest/Bridging from the Last Lesson and Prior Knowledge. What do the Students Already Know? Create the Experience

_____

_____

_____

Academic Language needed _____

_____

Materials needed

_____

Technology needed

_____

ISTE Standards Addressed

You must get your students ready to learn. You may plan an amazing lesson, but if the students are not ready to learn, then your lesson will be taught amiss! Your plans must include conducting an environmental scan. What will it take to motivate your students to want to learn?

Here are questions and considerations for teacher planning, but…do not get overwhelmed…this will become an automatic process!!!

1. *Are any of your students hungry?*

Keep crackers and fruit in your desk. Arrange with the cafeteria to help with late arrivals who miss breakfast. Follow District and school guidelines, especially with respect to food allergies.

2. *Have you planned for any students who are ill?*

Have tissues handy along with hand sanitizer. Have hall passes ready for students to visit the nurse.

3. *What about planning for signs of social emotional concerns…tears? Isolation? Unusual attention seeking? Anger?*

Social Emotional Learning SEL is an emerging area of study for teachers (CASEL, 2019).

4. *Do the students have the requisite skills for this lesson?*

Start with vocabulary. **Academic Language** refers to words, symbols, and functions needed to carry out the lesson successfully. (https://www.edglossary.org/academic-language/)

5. *What materials and technology will be needed*?

6. The creation of your lesson plan is a mental rehearsal for actual teaching.

7. Your classroom must be a model for respect and fairness. Trust will make it safe for the students to follow you as a leader. Create a sense of excitement! Create an environment that will invite students to be a part of something great. Create the experience for students who may lack a reference for the topic you are about to introduce. Technology is a good attention grabber and can mitigate gaps in experiences. You are the manager of your classroom, and your lesson plans should reflect it.

Lesson 3 The Beginning

Practice

Lesson Plan

Date___January 15, 2019_____

Teacher's Name _____ School _____ Class Time _____

Subject___Language Arts 5th grade_____

Focus of the Lesson and GSE Standard___ ELAGSE5RI2: Determine two or more main ideas of a text and explain how they are supported by key details; summarize the text. https://www.georgiastandards.org/Georgia-Standards/Frameworks/ELA-Grade-Five-Guidance.pdf

Class Announcements, Taking Roll, and Removal of all Barriers to Learning

Beginning—Introduction/Engagement/Grabbing Interest/Bridging from the Last Lesson and Prior Knowledge. What do the Students Already Know? Create the Experience

_____

_____

_____

Academic Language needed:

Discuss, compare, contrast, summarize, fiction, nonfiction, details

_____

Materials needed _____ https://books.apple.com/us/book/reading-comprehension-for-5th-grade-martin-luther-king/id588157848 _____

Technology needed For the teacher

_____

ISTE Standard Addressed
_____

Complete the missing components. The highlighted areas are completed for you.

NOTES for Lesson 3

Using the Cornell Model*

Key Words	Key Ideas

Summary:

*A design by Walter Paulk, a professor at Cornell University *Pauk, Walter; Owens, Ross J. Q. (2010). How to Study in College (10 ed.). Boston, MA: Wadsworth. ISBN 978-1-4390-8446-5*. Chapter 10: "The Cornell System: Take Effective Notes", pp. 235-277

LESSON 4

The Middle

Instructional Content

The middle of the lesson is the main part of teaching.

Middle—Methods, Activities, Steps

1. Communicate the focus of the day's lesson and purpose

2. Review the vocabulary, materials and resources needed to be successful

3. Present the new information—Differentiate with questioning and delivery. Ask what am I providing for those on grade level? Below grade level? Above grade level?

_____

_____

_____

_____

4. Model the appropriate response

5. Give opportunities for practice—Differentiate with the expected outcome

If you are using a scripted lesson, district lesson, or teacher's manual, use the steps provided. Lessons can be delivered in a whole group, flexible groups or even one-on-one. During this time, the teacher must know the content thoroughly. If you find that you are unsure of the content, stay two lessons ahead of your instruction with self-study. As you transition from teaching yourself, provide the steps for your lesson that helped you master understanding. Provide strategies for those who are struggling learners as well as learners who need a challenge.

With old school assessment, teaching was separate from assessment. Most of the time, testing followed teaching. Please read the difference between Assessment of Learning, and Assessment for Learning. What types of **formative assessment** can you insert in your lesson? (Stiggens, 2012). View this https://www.youtube.com/watch?v=EDVHuHyCGmg

Lesson 4 The Middle

Practice

The middle of the lesson is the main part of teaching.

Middle—Methods, Activities, Steps

1. Communicate the focus of the day's lesson and purpose

2. Review the vocabulary, materials and resources needed to be successful

3. Present the new information—Differentiate with questioning and delivery. Ask what am I providing for those on grade level? Below grade level? Above grade level?

_____

_____

_____

_____

_____

4. Model the appropriate response

5. Give opportunities for practice—Differentiate with the expected outcome

Explore this website: http://www.corestandards.org/ELA-Literacy/

Find a Common Core standard and build a lesson.

NOTES for Lesson 4

Using the Cornell Model*

Key Words	Key Ideas

Summary:

*A design by Walter Paulk, a professor at Cornell University *Pauk, Walter; Owens, Ross J. Q. (2010). How to Study in College (10 ed.). Boston, MA: Wadsworth. ISBN 978-1-4390-8446-5.* Chapter 10: "The Cornell System: Take Effective Notes", pp. 235-277

LESSON 5

The Ending

Instructional Content

How are you going to prove that learning occurred? The end of the lesson MUST include summarizing. It is also appropriate to provide **summative assessment**. According to Marzano (2001), summarizing is a high yield strategy. Obtain a copy of the strategies here: https://www.inflexion.org/marzanos-nine-high-yield-instructional-strategies/

Students should be able to explain what they have learned.

The end also includes reflective practice. The lesson plan is a living document. You will make notes on your plans that will facilitate planning in the future.

Lesson 5 The Ending

Practice

End—Closure and Summary of the Lesson

6. Are the students able to share what they learned?

7. Gather evidence of learning_____

8. Assign homework or some method of reinforcing the learning, as well as setting the stage for what is to come.

Reflection—Did the students learn the material? Why? Why not? What do I need to adjust? What ISTE Teacher Standard did you use while preparing and teaching this lesson? https://www.iste.org/standards/iste-standards-for-teachers

_____

_____

Respond to 6, 7, and 8. Prepare a reflection. Respond to a situation where three students were unsuccessful with the lesson. Explain how you will provide re-teaching in a **re-engagement lesson**.

NOTES for Lesson 5

Using the Cornell Model*

Key Words	Key Ideas

Summary:

*A design by Walter Paulk, a professor at Cornell University *Pauk, Walter; Owens, Ross J. Q. (2010). How to Study in College (10 ed.). Boston, MA: Wadsworth. ISBN 978-1-4390-84465.* Chapter 10: "The Cornell System: Take Effective Notes", pp. 235-277

LESSON 6

Pulling It All Together

Design a lesson plan using the provided template. First, let's study the rubric.

0	1	2	3
Missing key components in the Beginning, Middle and End	The lesson plan has partially developed components	The lesson plan has well-developed components of the following:	The lesson plan has three well-developed components that are coordinated
	The Beginning includes the focus of the lesson	The Beginning includes the focus, standard, and consideration for motivation	The Beginning includes the focus and a standard, and consideration for motivation

	The Middle includes the steps for a lesson	The Middle includes academic language, materials, technology, steps, and evidence of differentiation	The Middle includes academic language materials, technology, delivery mode and details, with evidence of differentiation using formative assessment
	The Ending includes the closing for the lesson	The Ending includes a summary, evidence of learning and reflection	The Ending includes a summary, assessment, evidence of learning and reflection

Lesson 6 Pulling it All Together

Lesson Plan

Date _____

Teacher's Name _____ School _____ Class Time _____

Subject _____

Focus of the Lesson and Standard (Purpose) _____

Class Announcements, Taking Roll, and Removal of all Barriers to Learning

Beginning--Introduction/Engagement/Grabbing Interest/Bridging from the Last Lesson and Prior Knowledge... What do the Students Already Know? Create the Experience

_____

_____

Academic Language needed _____

Materials needed _____

Technology needed _____

ISTE Standard Addressed: ISTE Standards: Educators | ISTE

_____

Middle--Methods, Activities, Steps

1. Communicate the focus of the day's lesson and purpose

2. Review the vocabulary, materials and resources needed to be successful

3. Present the new information—Differentiate with questioning and delivery _____

_____

4. Model the appropriate response

5. Give opportunities for practice—Differentiate with the expected outcome

End—Closure and Summary of the Lesson

1. Are the students able to share what they have learned?

2. Gather evidence of learning _____

_____

3. Assign homework or some method of reinforcing the learning, as well as, setting the stage for what is to come.

Reflection—Did the students learn the material? Why? Why not? What do I need to adjust? What ISTE Teacher Standard did you use while preparing and teaching this lesson? ISTE Standards: Educators | ISTE

_____

Summary

The purpose of *A Basic Guide to Lesson Planning for Teacher Candidates and Beginning Teachers* is to help provide a step-by-step process for teaching lesson planning. Please note that your employer may require a different format, but the basic components learned here should closely resemble any format, hence the labels: Beginning, Middle and End. Best wishes for a career in successful lesson planning. Give your students the best instruction by starting with the best plan!

Academic Language

Anticipatory Set

Assessment

Components

Culturally Responsive Pedagogy--CRP

Culturally Relevant Pedagogy--CRP

Design

Formative Assessment

ISTE Standards

Learning Segment

Lesson Plan

Objectives

Motivation

Module

Re-engagement lesson

Reflective Practice

Social Emotional Learning SEL

Standards

Summative Assessment

Unit

Bibliography

ASCD, 2019. Retrieved from http://www.ascd.org/whole-child.aspx

(CASEL, 2019) Retrieved from https://casel.org/what-is-sel/

Hunter, R. (2004). *Madeline Hunter's mastery teaching*. Thousand Oaks, CA: Corwin

Toward a Theory of Culturally Relevant Pedagogy

Gloria Ladson-Billings

First Published September 1, 1995 Research Article. Retrieved from https://doi.org/10.3102/00028312032003465

Gay, G. (2002). Preparing for culturally responsive teaching. Journal of Teacher Education, 53, 106–116.

Harris, T. (2019). The Right Tools: A Guide to Selecting, Evaluating, and Implementing Classroom Resources and Practices. Heinemann.

INTASC Standards (2019). Retrieved from https://ccsso.org/sites/default/files/2017-11/InTASC_Model_Core_Teaching_Standards_2011.pdf https://ccsso.org/resource-library/intasc-model-core-teaching-standards-and-learning-progressions-teachers-10

ITSE, 2019 Retrieved from https://www.iste.org/standards

Marzano, 2001. Classroom Instruction that Works: Research-based Strategies for Increasing Student Achievement.

Maslow, A.H. (1943). "A theory of human motivation". *Psychological Review*. **50** (4): 370–96. CiteSeerX 10.1.1.334.7586. doi:10.1037/h0054346 – via psychclassics.yorku.ca

(Ed. Glossary, 2013) Retrieved from https://www.edglossary.org/academic-language/
Schlechty, 2019. Retrieved from https://www.schlechtycenter.org/

Pauk, Walter; Owens, Ross J. Q. (2010). How to Study in College (10 ed.). Boston, MA: Wadsworth. ISBN 978-1-4390-8446-5. Chapter 10: "The Cornell System: Take Effective Notes", pp. 235-277

Stiggens, 2012. https://www.youtube.com/watch?v=EDVHuHyCGmg

www.ingramcontent.com/pod-product-compliance
Lightning Source LLC
Chambersburg PA
CBHW081651270326
41933CB00018B/3439